LEBRON JAMES

LEBRON JAMES

NBA Superstar and Activist

Heather E. Schwartz

LERNER PUBLICATIONS ◆ MINNEAPOLIS

Lerner Publications Company
An imprint of Lerner Publishing Group, Inc.
241 First Avenue North
Minneapolis, MN 55401 USA

For reading levels and more information, look up this title at www.lernerbooks.com.

Image credits: AP Photo/Marcio Jose Sanchez, p. 2; AP Photo/Tony Dejak, p. 6; Michael Macor/ San Francisco Chronicle/Getty Images, p. 9; Sean Pavone/Shutterstock.com, p. 10; LUCY NICHOLSON/AFP/Getty Images, p. 12; AF archive/Alamy Stock Photo, p. 14; Johnny Nunez/ WireImage/Getty Images, p. 15; AP Photo/John Swart, p. 16; AF archive/Alamy Stock Photo, p. 18; Ron Kuntz RK/REUTERS/Alamy Stock Photo, p. 20; AP Photo/Tony Dejak, p. 22; Shareif Ziyadat/FilmMagic/Getty Images, p. 24; JEFF HAYNES/AFP/Getty Images, p. 26; Jamie Squire/ Getty Images, p. 27; MARK RALSTON/AF/Getty Images, p. 28; AP Photo/Duane Burleson, p. 30; Ron Elkman/Sports Imager/Getty Images, p. 32; Christian Petersen/Getty Images, p. 35; Jeffrey Mayer/WireImage/Getty Images, p. 36; Justin Sullivan/Getty Images, p. 39; AP Photo/Mark Mulligan/Houston Chronicle, p. 40. Cover: Tinseltown/Shutterstock.com.

Main body text set in Rotis Serif Std 55 Regular. Typeface provided by Adobe Systems.

Designer: Lauren Cooper
Lerner team: Sue Marquis

Library of Congress Cataloging-in-Publication Data

Names: Schwartz, Heather E., author.
Title: LeBron James : NBA superstar and activist / Heather E. Schwartz.
Description: Minneapolis : Lerner Publications, MN, 2022. | Series: Gateway biographies |
    Includes bibliographical references and index. | Audience: Ages 9–14 | Audience: Grades 4–6
    | Summary: "Four-time NBA champion LeBron James has been a basketball superstar since
    high school. Learn about his journey to become an all-time NBA great and his life of activism
    off the court"— Provided by publisher.
Identifiers: LCCN 2021038043 (print) | LCCN 2021038044 (ebook) | ISBN 9781728441856 (library
    binding) | ISBN 9781728448770 (paperback) | ISBN 9781728444710 (ebook)
Subjects: LCSH: James, LeBron—Juvenile literature. | Basketball players—United States—
    Biography—Juvenile literature. | African American basketball players—Biography—Juvenile
    literature.
Classification: LCC GV884.J36 S45 2022 (print) | LCC GV884.J36 (ebook) | DDC 796.323092
    [B]—dc23

LC record available at https://lccn.loc.gov/2021038043
LC ebook record available at https://lccn.loc.gov/2021038044

Manufactured in the United States of America
1-49940-49783-9/28/2021

TABLE OF CONTENTS

LeBron James keeps the ball away from a Golden State Warriors defender during Game 3 of the 2016 National Basketball Association Finals. James scored 32 points to lead the Cleveland Cavaliers to a 30-point win.

n June 2016, the Cleveland Cavaliers took on the Golden State Warriors in the National Basketball Association (NBA) Finals. Cleveland's best player, LeBron James, had one goal in mind. He wanted to lead his team to their first NBA championship. After four seasons with the Miami Heat, he'd rejoined the Cavs after the 2013–2014 season to do exactly that.

The Cavs needed to win four out of seven games in the series to take the championship, but the odds were against them. After Game 4, the Warriors led the series 3–1. No team had ever trailed 3–1 and come back to win the Finals, but James and the Cavs were determined to make history.

In Game 5, James scored 41 points in a 112–97 Cleveland victory. Three days later, he scored 41 again to help beat Golden State 115–101. The Cavs had come back to tie the series, but they needed to win the next game to make it count.

Game 7 was at Oracle Arena in Oakland, California. With the score tied 89–89 and 1:50 left on the game clock, James made one of the biggest defensive plays of his career. The Warriors raced down the court with the ball. Golden State superstar Steph Curry passed to his teammate Andre Iguodala, who had a clear path to score. As Iguodala jumped to lay the ball into the basket, James came soaring from behind him. James batted the ball against the backboard, causing it to bounce away from the basket and into the hands of a teammate.

The incredible defensive play kept the score tied. With less than one minute left in the game, Cleveland's Kyrie Irving sank a 25-foot (7.6 m) three-point shot to give the Cavs the lead. After the Warriors missed a shot at the other end of the court, they fouled James. He made one of his free throws to put the Cavs ahead 93–89. Golden State missed two more shots, and the Cavs became NBA champions.

Cleveland fans at the arena cheered for their team's first NBA championship. Cavaliers coach Tyronn Lue wept tears of joy. James was so overcome with emotion that he could barely speak. "I gave everything that I had," he said. "I put my heart, my blood, my sweat, my tears into this game. . . . Cleveland, this is for you!"

James holds the Larry O'Brien NBA Championship Trophy after helping the Cavaliers defeat the Warriors in 2016.

A ROUGH START

LeBron James was born on December 30, 1984, in Akron, Ohio. His mother, Gloria, was 16 when he was born, so they lived with her mother and grandmother in a big house in Akron. LeBron's father was absent from his life and didn't help raise him. His mother's partner, Eddie Jackson, who LeBron considered to be his father, was in prison at that time. LeBron's grandmother and great-grandmother looked after him while his mother went to school.

Akron is in Northeast Ohio, just south of Cleveland.

When LeBron was three, his grandmother and great-grandmother both died. Even with help from LeBron's uncles, his mother couldn't manage the house. It was too expensive to heat and maintain. When a neighbor came over to visit, she noticed how cold the house was and saw a hole in the living room floor. She said it was dangerous to live there and invited LeBron and his mother to stay with her.

From then on, the two didn't have a real home of their own. They spent a few months sleeping on the couch at the neighbor's house. Then they moved on to live with other friends and relatives, never staying in one place for long. LeBron's life was unstable in other ways too. His mother didn't always supervise him. When he was in fourth grade, she sometimes left him home alone at night so she could go out with her friends. During the day, he often skipped school to play video games. The neighborhoods where he grew up were dangerous. "I saw drugs, guns, killings; it was crazy," LeBron said. "But my mom kept food in my mouth and clothes on my back."

When LeBron was nine, however, something happened that would put him on a new path. He and his mother were staying with a friend in an apartment building for people with low incomes. One day, LeBron was outside playing tag with friends when Bruce Kelker, a youth football coach, came by. Kelker wanted to create a winning team, and he was looking for players. He asked LeBron and his friends if they might like to join.

The coach had the kids run a 100-yard (91 m) footrace to compete for the position of running back. He was impressed when LeBron won by 15 yards (14 m). Gloria wasn't sure about having him join a football team. She worried about the costs for equipment and difficulties getting him to team practices without a car. But Kelker promised he'd take care of everything. He had to have LeBron on his team, the East Dragons.

LeBron's mother holds a sign with his face printed on it during a basketball game. He said his mother gave him all the support he needed.

Playing football changed LeBron's life. He had something to do on the weekends, since he had to show up for games. He gained friendships with teammates who respected his talent on the field. His relationship with Kelker was also important. The coach was an adult LeBron could count on, in addition to his mom.

Since Kelker was picking up LeBron for practices and games, he couldn't help noticing how often LeBron and his mother moved. Kelker soon invited them to live with him. They stayed for a few months before Gloria James began looking for a new place to stay. She was still wondering where to go next when another youth football coach, Frank Walker, invited LeBron to live with his family.

LeBron started living with the Walkers while his mother stayed with a friend and saw her son on the weekends. At the Walkers', LeBron had more stability than he'd ever known. Walker and his wife had three children and treated LeBron like one of their own. They gave him chores to do and made sure he went to school and did his homework. "It changed my life," LeBron said. "The next year I had perfect attendance and a B average."

When football season ended, Walker signed LeBron up for basketball. LeBron played on a team for nine-year-olds and was an assistant coach for an eight-year-old team. In a very short time, he'd made big changes in his life. He was no longer the kid who ditched school to play video games. He was learning new ways to live and playing healthier games that improved his confidence. Not only that, he'd found his sport—and it wasn't football.

LeBron (*second from right*) celebrates a win with his teammates.

GROWING UP

Around the time that LeBron was in sixth grade, Eddie Jackson left prison. He stepped in as LeBron's father and helped support the family. LeBron started spending more time with his mother and Eddie, though he still lived with the Walkers part-time.

LeBron also continued playing basketball. By eighth grade, it was clear he was a standout player. He led his team to the championship game at a youth national tournament. When he entered St. Vincent-St. Mary

(SVSM) High School in Akron, he was tall and strong, and his basketball career took off. As a freshman in 1999–2000, he averaged 21 points per game. The team didn't lose all year and won the state title. They couldn't have done it without LeBron.

The following year, he was even better. LeBron led his high school team to win the state championship again. He was the first sophomore player to win Ohio's Mr. Basketball award as the best high school player in

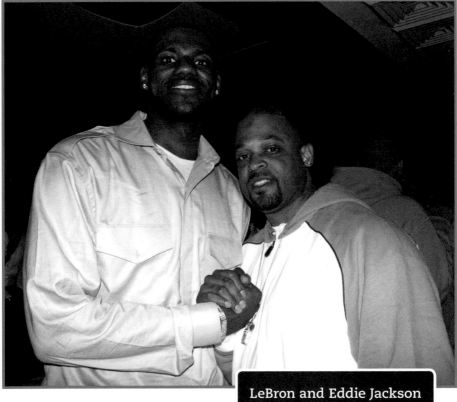

LeBron and Eddie Jackson after a game in 2006

the state. During the summer, he played at the ABCD Basketball Camp for youth and won an award as the most valuable player.

Fans, scouts, professional players, and coaches couldn't help but notice the teen sensation. Michael Jordan, who many fans consider to be the greatest basketball player of all time, invited LeBron to workout sessions in Chicago, Illinois. LeBron also formed friendships with NBA stars such as Antoine Walker, Michael Finley, Tracy McGrady, and Jerry Stackhouse.

Michael Jordan soars for a slam dunk in 1988. He won six NBA championships with the Chicago Bulls.

LeBron's basketball talent was astonishing, and he also earned respect for his unselfish attitude and ability to predict the flow of the game on the court. LeBron was special, and even he had a hard time explaining it. "A lot of players know how to play the game, but they really don't know how to play the game, if you know what I mean," LeBron said. "They can put the ball in the hoop, but I see things before they even happen."

When LeBron was 17, he appeared on the February 18, 2002, cover of *Sports Illustrated*. Printed in big white letters on the cover were the words, "The Chosen One." And the honors and big games kept coming. He scored 50 points in one game. Then he scored 52 points in a game SVSM won 78–52. That meant he'd scored as many points alone as the opposing team scored in total. He averaged more than 30 points per game as a senior in 2002–2003. For the third time since he joined the school, SVSM won the state title.

KING JAMES

LeBron had a nickname in high school that has stuck with him throughout his career: King James. No one knows who first started calling him King James. Most of his fans say the media gave him the name. Others believe he gave it to himself. But no matter where the nickname came from, it fits. LeBron means "king" in some languages spoken in Africa.

LeBron (*second from left*) poses with some of his SVSM teammates. He made several lifelong friendships in high school.

In both 2002 and 2003, LeBron was named Gatorade Player of the Year, an award given to the best high school athlete in a sport in the United States. He was the first person to ever win the award twice. After his junior year, he considered challenging NBA rules to start playing professionally, but ultimately he decided to finish high school first. "The rule's not fair, but that's life," he said. "I'll stay another year because my friends are here."

NBA ELIGIBILITY

The eligibility rules for the NBA Draft have changed over time. When LeBron attended SVSM, the league did not allow players to join until their class had graduated from high school. In 2006 the NBA changed the rules to make players wait even longer. The new guidelines stated that players had to be at least 19 during their draft year, and they had to have graduated from high school at least one year ago.

When the rules changed in 2006, then commissioner of the NBA David Stern said the draft eligibility guidelines improved the quality of the league. He said that teenagers weren't physically and emotionally mature enough to handle the league's tough play and the money that came with an NBA contract. But critics said that the new rules were all about saving money for team owners. By limiting the number of years players could be in the league, owners also limited the amount of money they had to pay those players.

Basketball fans couldn't get enough of LeBron. Some of his high school games appeared on nationwide TV in the United States.

LeBron had a big future ahead, but staying in high school for one more year had some advantages. Though his schedule kept him busy, he still made time for a personal life. Throughout high school, he dated classmate Savannah Brinson. On their first date, they went to a steak house for dinner, and when he drove her home, she forgot to take her leftovers from his car. LeBron went back to her house to deliver them. Savannah later joked that he was probably just making an excuse to see her again.

GOING PRO

James considered going to college after high school. He told people that big-time basketball universities such as Duke, Ohio State, North Carolina, Florida, and Louisville were on his list. But no one was surprised when he decided to go straight into the NBA Draft instead.

With his fame about to explode, major corporations courted James to endorse their products. They tried to woo him with private jet rides, parties and, of course, money. Adidas offered James $60 million, Nike $87 million, and Reebok $115 million. But James didn't base his choice solely on cash. He wanted to be with a company that would make amazing commercials and shoe designs that would become part of his legacy. He thought it over and decided Nike was the right partner. When he signed the contract paperwork on May 22, 2003, he locked in a seven-year endorsement deal. Nike rewarded him with a bonus check for $10 million.

The next day, James was the top pick in the NBA Draft. The Cavaliers had the first pick and quickly snapped up the star player. James was excited to stay in Ohio and looked forward to helping the Cavs improve. During the 2002–2003 season, Cleveland had tied for the worst record in the NBA at 17–65.

James scored 25 points in his NBA debut against the Sacramento Kings on October 29, 2003, but Cleveland lost by 14 points. With their new star player leading the way, the 2003–2004 Cavaliers slowly began to get better. They ended the season at 35–47, a huge improvement over the previous year. James won the Rookie of the Year award.

Jumping straight from high school to the NBA was rare because most players couldn't handle the steep and sudden increase in competition. For the first time in his life, James wasn't always the best player on the court. He survived by staying true to himself and working really hard. "If you've got a great work ethic, you can survive in this league," he said.

James's whole life had changed, and he recognized that he had become a role model like other professional basketball players had been to him. In 2004 he founded the LeBron James Family Foundation to serve kids in Akron. Its aim is to support education and help at-risk students succeed. In addition to a school and a sports and recreation facility, the foundation also built affordable housing in Akron. James was thrilled to be able to give back to his community. He remembered how hard it had been to grow up with little money and no steady home.

James holds up his new jersey after the Cavaliers chose him with the first overall pick in the 2003 NBA Draft.

James also had victories in both his personal and professional life in 2004. He and Savannah attended her high school prom together. During the summer, he went to Athens, Greece, to play for Team USA at the Olympic Games, where they won a bronze medal. In October James became a father when he and Savannah had a son, LeBron Jr.

At 18, life was a whirlwind for James. But for all his success, his NBA career was just beginning. It seemed like nothing could stop him.

LEADING THE CAVALIERS

The 2004–2005 season ended without a championship win for the Cavs, but the team improved its record again, finishing the year 42–40. James was the team's leading scorer that year, ranking third in the league in points per game behind Kobe Bryant of the Los Angeles Lakers and Allen Iverson of the Philadelphia 76ers. The following year, James was his team's top scorer again. At the end of that season, Cleveland made it to the playoffs for the first time in eight years. They beat the Washington Wizards in the first round before falling to the Detroit Pistons.

James was leading the Cavs through the 2006–2007 season when talk turned to the upcoming Summer Olympics. To play in the Olympics, James would have to commit to a qualifying tournament in Las Vegas, Nevada, after the NBA season. He was hesitant, and that didn't sit well with Team USA's managing director. But James had other priorities in addition to basketball and a good reason to make a careful decision with his family's needs in mind. "Right now, I'm 50–50 [on playing in the qualifying tournament]," James said. "My girlfriend is expecting another [baby] in June. Health is always an issue. You have to re-evaluate things, go through the season, go through the playoffs and then look at it afterward."

James and Savannah Brinson attend an awards show.

The Cavs finished the season with a 50–32 record, second best in the Eastern Conference. In the playoffs, they beat three teams to reach the NBA Finals. But in the championship series against the San Antonio Spurs, Cleveland lost the first three games. The Cavs were preparing for Game 4 when Savannah went into labor. James spent most of the night at the hospital with her. On June 14, 2007, they welcomed their second son, Bryce Maximus James.

WORKING HIS GIFTS

Body size and natural talent are big parts of James's success. He is 6 feet 9 (2 m) and weighs 250 pounds (113 kg). He can run faster than most players his size, and he jumps higher and stays in the air longer. He can spin and turn more quickly. But he doesn't owe all of his success to his physical gifts. His career depends on his body, and James works hard to keep it running.

During the NBA season, James exercises every day, often rising at 5 a.m. to begin his workouts. A normal day begins with icing and stretching his muscles to keep them loose and prevent injury. He also does yoga to strengthen and stretch his muscles. After that, James may head to the gym to lift weights. On other days, he goes to the basketball court where he shoots, dribbles, and practices all the skills he needs during games. He works out five to seven days a week during the off-season too.

The next day, James was back on the court with the Cavaliers, and fans hoped the birth of his son might bring them some luck. The team was in a three-game hole, and their chances to win a championship weren't looking good. James led his team in scoring, but the Cavs lost by one point. He carried the loss with him for years and used it as motivation. "[The Spurs] beat us on our home floor, celebrated on our home floor," James said. "I won't forget that."

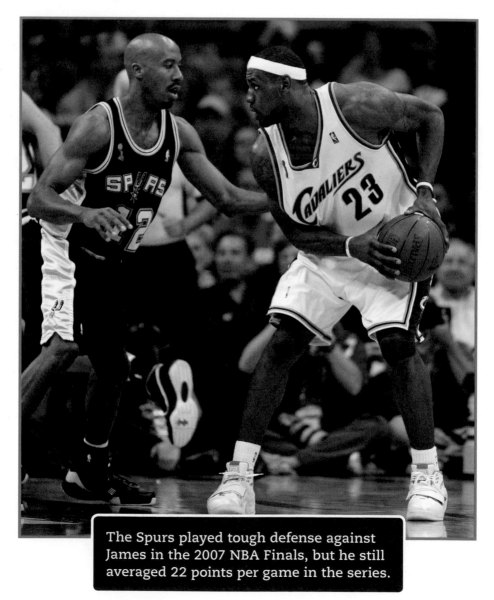

The Spurs played tough defense against James in the 2007 NBA Finals, but he still averaged 22 points per game in the series.

That summer James decided to play in the tournament that qualified him for his second Olympic Games. In 2008 he traveled to Beijing, China, to play for Team USA. The team was carefully selected to include players with different strengths. Along with star players Kobe Bryant, Dwyane Wade, and Chris Bosh, James helped the team take home a gold medal.

By 2009 James was a 24-year-old with a highly unusual life story to tell. He got to work with a Pulitzer Prize–winning journalist, Buzz Bissinger, to write about his life and experiences. Together, they wrote *Shooting Stars*. The book gave fans new insights into James's childhood in Akron and the mistakes he'd made as a high school student.

James had realized many of his dreams with the Cavaliers, but one was still out of reach. He hadn't won an NBA

James puts up a shot against Spain in the gold medal game at the 2008 Olympics. He, Dwyane Wade, and Kobe Bryant led the team in scoring.

championship. After the 2009–2010 season, he made an announcement. He was leaving Cleveland to pursue a championship with the Miami Heat. It wasn't an easy decision. "At the end of the day, I feel awful," James said. "I feel even worse that I wasn't able to bring an NBA championship to [Cleveland]. I never wanted to leave Cleveland. My heart will always be around that area."

When James joined the Heat, he created a lot of excitement with fans in Miami. The day after his announcement, the team sold all of their available season tickets.

A FRESH START IN MIAMI

When James left the Cavaliers, some were outraged. The team's owner called his decision a betrayal. Some Cleveland fans burned their James jerseys. But James knew he had to do what would make him happy. He wanted an NBA championship, and he thought his new Heat teammates could help him get it.

THE DECISION

When James announced that he was leaving the Cavs, it didn't go over well with his teammates and many of his fans. One reason for the icy reception was the way James delivered the news. Without telling his team ahead of time, he blurted out the news on TV. The show, *The Decision*, was his agent's idea, and James went along with it as a way to raise money for charity. The show raised about $3 million for the Boys and Girls Clubs of America.

In Miami, James was joining a team that already included Dwyane Wade and Chris Bosh, star players who'd helped Team USA take home the gold medal at the 2008 Summer Olympics. James hoped that along with Wade and Bosh, he'd be able to lead the Heat to the title. But he knew they'd need the whole team to get there. "A team and a championship team is not built on just three guys or just one superstar," James said. "It's built on the whole organization and everybody having the same goal and the same goal in mind."

James displayed a message on his shoe honoring Trayvon Martin during a game in 2012.

In James's first season in Miami, the Heat won the Southeast Division and made it to the 2011 NBA Finals. They fell to the Dallas Mavericks in six games. But that same year, James had a victory off the court. At the end of 2011, he brought a $300,000 diamond ring with him to a New Year's Eve party. He asked Wade to hold it for him. Then, when the ball dropped at midnight, James asked Savannah to marry him. It was a milestone moment with the woman he'd loved since long before his professional basketball days. Despite their long history, he was nervous about proposing. But James had nothing to worry about with Savannah. She accepted the ring and said yes right away. "Savannah was with me shooting in the gym when I [had] absolutely nothing," he said. "[Savannah] was down when I was at my high school, no cameras, no lights. And she was there with me."

The engagement kicked off a year of change, growth, and dreams achieved for James. In early 2012, he was outraged when the media began reporting on Trayvon Martin, a Black teenager who was shot and killed by a neighborhood watch member in Florida. The shooter, George Zimmerman, wasn't charged with a crime for more than a month. James felt strongly about the situation and spoke out about it. "Having kids of my own—having boys of my own—it hit home for me to see and to learn the story and to think that if my boy left home and he never returned," he said. "That kinda hit a switch. From that point on, I knew that my voice and my platform had to be used for more than just sports."

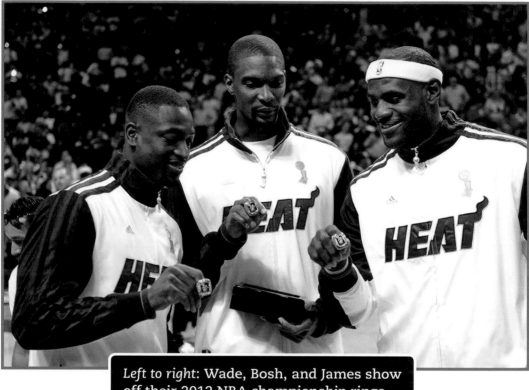

Left to right: Wade, Bosh, and James show off their 2012 NBA championship rings.

At the end of the 2011–2012 season, James got the championship he'd always wanted. The Heat beat the Oklahoma City Thunder in the NBA Finals. That moment met all of James's expectations, and he felt he'd reached a lifelong dream.

That summer James played for Team USA at the 2012 Olympic Games in London, England. Wade and Bosh were no longer on the team. But James and his teammates, including James Harden and Kevin Durant, won another gold medal.

HOW THE NBA PLAYOFFS WORK

The NBA has two conferences, the Eastern Conference and the Western Conference. The top eight teams in each conference participate in the playoffs and play best-of-seven series to advance. Teams start by playing in the West First Round and the East First Round. Winners advance to the Western Conference Semifinals and the Eastern Conference Semifinals. The two conference finals are next. Finally, the last two surviving teams go toe to toe in the NBA Finals.

RETURNING TO HIS ROOTS

In 2013 the Heat won the NBA championship again. Later that year, on September 14, James and Savannah wed. Their wedding was a three-day celebration at the Capella Chapel Grand Del Mar hotel in San Diego, California. They hosted more than 200 friends and family, including Dwyane Wade and rapper Jay-Z.

SPORTS STAR TO MOVIE STAR

James has thrilled basketball fans for decades, and his fame has given him many other opportunities to entertain people throughout his long career. He appeared as a guest on TV shows like *Good Morning America* and *The Tonight Show Starring Jimmy Fallon*, and he hosted *Saturday Night Live* in September 2007. He even voiced a character based on himself for an episode of *The Simpsons*.

James has made it to the big screen too. When he played himself in the 2015 movie *Trainwreck*, some critics said he stole the show. In 2021 James starred in the movie *Space Jam: A New Legacy*. The movie was a sequel to the 1996 film *Space Jam* starring NBA megastar Michael Jordan.

In 2014 the Heat reached the NBA Finals for the third season in a row. They lost to the San Antonio Spurs, and James decided to shake up his career once again. He announced he was taking advantage of an option in his contract to leave the Heat. That meant also walking away from the $20.6 million his contract promised if he stayed for the following season. James knew he could earn even more with another team, but his decision to leave wasn't only about money. As a free agent, he could choose to join any team in the league.

By July, James knew where he belonged: back in Cleveland. "Our city hasn't had that [championship] feeling in a long, long, long time," he said. "My goal is still to win as many titles as possible, no question. But what's most important for me is bringing one trophy back to Northeast Ohio."

This time, Miami fans mourned while

James looks for an open teammate to pass the ball to during a 2015 game against the Phoenix Suns.

Cleveland fans celebrated. But the real celebration would come if and when James could help lead the team to a championship. That fall James became a father for the third time on October 22, 2014. He'd kept his wife's pregnancy mostly private throughout the year. He said he felt blessed to add their daughter, Zhuri James, to the family.

James and his wife have three children: LeBron Jr., Bryce Maximus, and Zhuri.

During the 2014–2015 season in Cleveland, James reaped some major off-the-court rewards when he signed a lifetime endorsement contract with Nike. At the time, the details of the contract weren't reported. But analysts later said that James might earn more than $1 billion in the deal.

On the court, James instantly made the Cavs a better team. They won the Central Division and then beat three teams in the playoffs to reach the

NBA Finals. They lost to the Golden State Warriors, but at the end of the 2015–2016 season, things were different. After 52 seasons without a championship, the Cavaliers beat the Warriors 93–89 in Game 7 of the Finals to take the NBA title. Three days later, more than one million people attended a celebratory parade through downtown Cleveland. James had given everything he had to bring his city a championship, and his efforts had paid off. The victory was proof that he'd made the right decision by returning to Cleveland.

FUTURE NFL STAR?

Throughout his career, fans have wondered whether James might one day play professional football. He loved football as a kid, and he has already proven to have plenty of sports talent. Many fans think the NBA superstar's speed, size, and strength could make him a star in the NFL too. In 2015, however, James put the rumors to rest and said he would not be playing professional football. "Love it still though," he wrote on Twitter.

RAISING HIS VOICE

After James and the Cavs won the NBA title, his place as a basketball legend was secure. But he felt he had more work to do in Cleveland. His return wasn't only about winning on the court. He also wanted to help kids in Ohio whose families didn't have much money and show them they had a future filled with promise.

In 2016 more than 1,000 students were going through the I Promise program supported by the LeBron James Family Foundation. I Promise provides mentors and other support to help students stay in school and succeed. It was a good start, but James wanted to do even more, and he wanted to make sure the country's highest leader supported him and the kids he wanted to help. In late 2016, James announced that he was endorsing presidential candidate Hillary Clinton in her run against Donald Trump.

James campaigned with Clinton when she traveled to Cleveland in November. As someone who grew up nearby, he could relate to voters and understand their concerns. He urged Ohioans to recognize that their vote counted and to use it to elect Clinton.

On the campaign trail, people clapped and cheered. But James's views weren't popular with everyone in the US, and he experienced hate and racism. In 2017 someone spray-painted a racist slur on the gates of his home. James was horrified but far from silenced. He told the media that his family's safety came first, but the incident opened an important conversation that he wanted to keep going.

James appears onstage with Hillary Clinton during a presidential campaign event.

"No matter how much money you have, no matter how famous you are, no matter how many people admire you, being Black in America is—it's tough," James said. "And we got a long way to go for us as a society and for us as African-Americans until we feel equal in America."

James wasn't just becoming more vocal about politics and issues involving racism. He was also taking action. In 2018 he opened the I Promise School in Akron. The school serves third through 10th grade students who need extra help with their schoolwork and attendance. Two years later, he joined other athletes and entertainers to start

After the 2020–2021 season, James ranked third on the NBA's career scoring list with 35,367 points. If he keeps playing for a few more seasons, he'll pass Karl Malone and Kareem Abdul-Jabbar to become the league's all-time highest scorer.

More Than a Vote, a group that encourages Black people and other people of color to vote by providing help and information about voting.

While James was making headlines for putting his fame and money to good use, he continued to win in the NBA, and the media continued to follow his career. In 2017 and 2018, Cleveland advanced to the NBA Finals, but they lost both series to the Warriors. Between Miami and Cleveland, James had played in the Finals an incredible eight years in a row. But his next move marked an end to his Finals streak.

In July 2018, James left the Cavaliers for the Los Angeles Lakers. The Lakers are one of the most famous and successful teams in sports, but they had missed the playoffs five years in a row. James hoped to help them return to their winning ways. He signed a four-year, $154 million contract with the team.

The Lakers didn't make it to the NBA Finals in 2019, breaking James's eight-season streak. But in 2020, he and fellow superstar Anthony Davis led Los Angeles to the NBA's championship series. They beat Miami in six games to claim the title. James became an NBA champion for the fourth time, and he won his fourth Finals Most Valuable Player Award.

By 2021 James had played in 17 NBA All-Star Games and won the NBA Most Valuable Player Award four times. After almost 20 seasons, he was one of the oldest players in the league, and still one of the best. He has been known as King James since his early days in high school, and his reign as the king of the NBA is expected to continue for years.

IMPORTANT DATES

 1984 LeBron James is born in Akron, Ohio.

 2002 James appears on the cover of *Sports Illustrated* with the headline "The Chosen One."

 2003 James joins the Cleveland Cavaliers.

 2004 James wins the NBA Rookie of the Year award.

He starts the LeBron James Family Foundation.

 2010 James joins the Miami Heat.

 2012 He wins his first NBA championship.

 2013 He marries Savannah Brinson.

2014 James returns to the Cavaliers.

 2015 He signs a lifetime contract with Nike.

 2016 James leads the Cavaliers to their first NBA championship.

 2018 James joins the Los Angeles Lakers.

He opens the I Promise School.

 2020 James leads the Lakers to victory in the NBA Finals and wins his fourth Finals Most Valuable Player award.

SOURCE NOTES

8   "LeBron James Postgame Interview–Cleveland Cavaliers Win the 2016 NBA Championship," YouTube video, 2:06, posted by Hoop Center, June 19, 2016, https://www.youtube.com/watch?v=3o_4fKmD6eo.

11   Grant Wahl, "Ahead of His Class," *Sports Illustrated* Vault, February 18, 2002, https://vault.si.com/vault/2002/02/18/ahead-of-his-class-ohio-high-school-junior-lebron-james-is-so-good-that-hes-already-being-mentioned-as-the-heir-to-air-jordan.

13   Wahl.

16–17 Wahl.

18   Wahl.

22   "LeBron James Rookie of the Year Press Conference," Cleveland Cavaliers, April 21, 2004, https://www.nba.com/cavaliers/news/roy_press_conference.html.

24   Chris Sheridan, "Team USA Update: Waffling by LeBron Irks Colangelo," *ESPN*, April 3, 2007, https://www.espn.com/nba/news/story?id=2824500.

26   Eric Freeman, "LeBron James Has Not Forgotten the 2007 Finals against the Spurs That Most of Us Have Forgotten," Yahoo! Sports, June 5, 2013, https://sports.yahoo.com/lebron-james-not-forgotten-2007-finals-against-spurs-220511971.html?y20=1.

28   "James Picks Heat; Cavs Owner Erupts," *ESPN*, July 8, 2010, https://www.espn.com/nba/news/story?id=5365165.

30   "James Picks Heat."

31 Selena Barrientos, "Inside LeBron James and His Wife Savannah Brinson's Incredible Love Story," *Good Housekeeping*, July 15, 2021, https://www.goodhousekeeping.com/life/entertainment/a34221477/lebron-james-wife-savannah-brinsons-marriage-kids/.

31 Antoinette Bueno, "How LeBron James Has Become a Powerful Voice for Activism on and off the Court," *ET*, July 1, 2020, https://www.etonline.com/how-lebron-james-has-become-a-powerful-voice-for-activism-on-and-off-the-court-148930.

35 LeBron James, as told to Lee Jenkins, "LeBron: I'm Coming Back to Cleveland," *Sports Illustrated*, July 11, 2014, https://www.si.com/nba/2014/07/11/lebron-james-cleveland-cavaliers.

37 Mark Sandritter, "10 Important Things We Learned from LeBron James' Twitter Q&A," SBNation, July 28, 2015, https://www.sbnation.com/lookit/2015/7/28/9064381/lebron-james-twitter-space-jam-2-kevin-love-ronda-rousey.

39 Scott Cacciola and Jonah Engel Bromwich, "LeBron James Responds to Racial Vandalism: 'Being Black in America Is Tough,'" *New York Times*, May 31, 2017, https://www.nytimes.com/2017/05/31/sports/lebron-racist-graffiti-home.html.

SELECTED BIBLIOGRAPHY

Blasi, Weston. "When LeBron James Chose Nike in 2003, He Gave Up $28 Million—It Could End Up Making Him $1 Billion." MarketWatch, September 1, 2019. https://www.marketwatch.com/story/when -lebron-james-chose-nike-in-2003-he-gave-up-28-million-it-could -end-up-making-him-1-billion-2019-08-29.

Cacciola, Scott, and Jonah Engel Bromwich. "LeBron James Responds to Racial Vandalism: 'Being Black in America Is Tough.'" *New York Times*, May 31, 2017. https://www.nytimes.com/2017/05/31/sports /lebron-racist-graffiti-home.html.

Klayman, Ben. "Kobe Bryant, LeBron James Head Olympic Basketball Team." Reuters, June 23, 2008. https://www.reuters.com/article /us-olympics-basketball-us/kobe-bryant-lebron-james-head-olympic -basketball-team-idUSN2041376820080623.

"LeBron James: Akron, Ohio's 'Shooting Star.'" NPR, September 15, 2009. https://www.npr.org/templates/story/story.php?storyId=112856567.

Taylor, Ihsan. "The King James Version." *New York Times*, October 1, 2009. https://www.nytimes.com/2009/10/04/books/review/Taylor-t .html.

"Top Moments: Cavs End Cleveland's Long Championship Drought." NBA, October 24, 2018. https://www.nba.com/history/top-moments /cleveland-cavaliers-win-title-2016.

LEARN MORE

Aretha, David. *LeBron vs. Durant vs. Curry vs. Jordan*. New York: Rosen, 2020.

LeBron James
https://www.lebronjames.com

LeBron James Family Foundation
https://www.lebronjamesfamilyfoundation.org

LeBron James—NBA.com
https://www.nba.com/player/2544/lebron_james

Levit, Joe. *Basketball's G.O.A.T.: Michael Jordan, LeBron James, and More*. Minneapolis: Lerner Publications, 2020.

Parker, Donald. *LeBron James*. Hollywood, FL: Mason Crest, 2022.

INDEX